Helping Children See Jesus

ISBN: 978-1-64104-064-8

The Priesthood Of Christ
New Testament Volume 36:
Hebrews, Part Three

Authors: R. Iona Lyster, Doris Stuber Moose, Maureen Pruitt
Illustrator: Frances H. Hertzler
Colorization Courtesy of Good Life Ministries
Page Layout: Patricia Pope

© 2019 Bible Visuals International
PO Box 153, Akron, PA 17501-0153
Phone: (717) 859-1131
www.biblevisuals.org

All rights reserved. No part of this publication may be reproduced, stored in a retrieval system or transmitted in any form by any means, electronic, mechanical, photocopy, recording or otherwise, without the prior permission of the publisher, except as provided by USA copyright law.

RELATED ITEMS

To access related items (such as activities, memory verse posters and translated texts) please visit our webstore at www.biblevisuals.org and enter 1036 in the search box on the page.

FREE TEXT DOWNLOAD

To access a FREE printable copy of the teaching text (PDF format) in English or other available languages, enter S1036DL in the search box. Add the item to your cart, and use coupon code XTACSV17 at checkout. Once your order is processed you will receive an email with a link to the free download.

STUDENT ACTIVITES

These are included with the FREE printable copy of the English teaching text for this story. See the directions under Free Text Download (above) to access them.

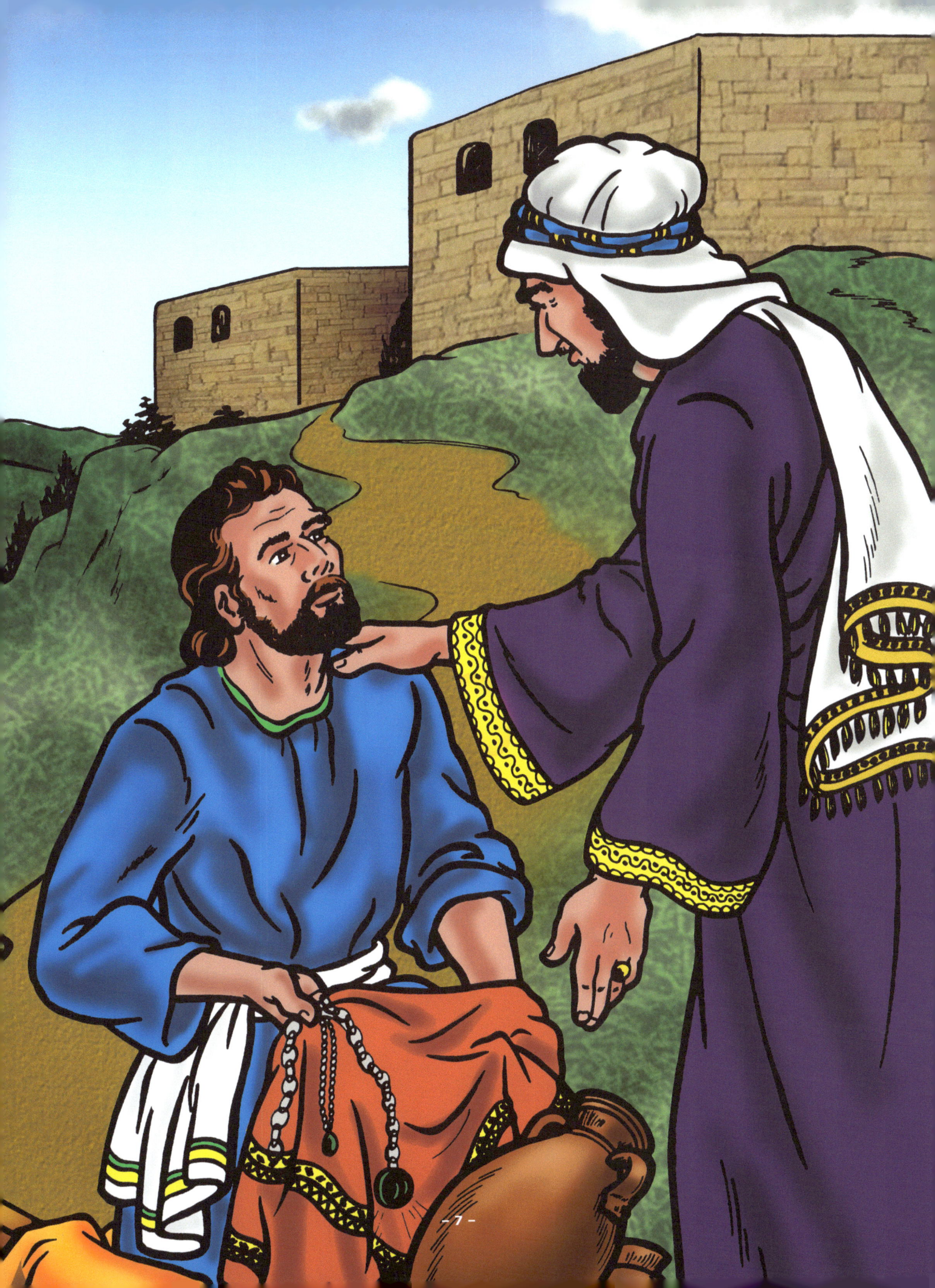

Seeing that we have a Great High Priest, that is passed into the heavens, Jesus, the Son of God, let us hold fast to our profession. Hebrews 4:14

Lesson 1
THE PRIESTHOOD OF AARON

> **NOTE TO THE TEACHER**
>
> A priest speaks to God for the people. He must be satisfactory to God if he is to go into the presence of God. Therefore, it is necessary that God choose His priests.
>
> Hebrews 5:4 says: "No man taketh this honor unto himself, but he that is called of God, as was Aaron."
>
> In this lesson we shall see that every believer is a priest to God. To be a priest, a person must be chosen by God. He says of believers: "You are a chosen generation, a royal priesthood (1 Peter 2:9). The Lord taught His disciples: "You have not chosen me, but I have chosen you . . . that you should go and bring forth fruit" (John 15:16). The Lord also told His disciples: "I have chosen you out of the world, therefore the world hates you" (John 15:19).
>
> Our Great High Priest was hated by the world. Yet "He learned obedience by the things which He suffered." (See Hebrews 5:8.) He knows and sympathizes with us as *we* learn obedience by the things which we suffer. Are you willing to be faithful to Him who has called you to be His priest?
>
> The ephod illustrated on pages 4 and 12 should have additional color. According to God's Word it was gold, blue, purple and scarlet.

Scripture to be studied: Exodus 19:5-8; 28:1–29:46; Leviticus 8:1-36; Hebrews 5:1-10; 7:11-28

The *aim* of the lesson: To lay a foundation for the study of the better priesthood of Christ and the priesthood of all believers.

What your students should *know*: Believers are priests to God.

What your students should *feel*: Responsible for living dedicated lives.

What your students should *do*: Dedicate themselves to serve God.

Lesson outline (for the teacher's and students' notebooks):

1. The priesthood: what it is (Hebrews 5:1-10; 7:11-28).
2. The reason for the priesthood (Romans 5:12-19).
3. God gives a priest to His people (Exodus 19:5-8).
4. God consecrates His priests (Exodus 28:1–29:46; Leviticus 8:1-36).

The verse to be memorized:

Seeing then that we have a great High Priest, that is passed into the heavens, Jesus, the Son of God, let us hold fast our profession. (Hebrews 4:14)

THE LESSON

John and his classmates were playing a fast game of kickball in the school yard. Their teacher explained, "I must go inside for a few minutes. You may continue with the game. But please stay away from the flowers we planted."

The children meant to obey. But soon the ball was kicked out of bounds close to the flower bed. Several boys scrambled for the ball. While fighting each other for it, four of them fell into the flowers, crushing all of them.

The children felt dreadful. They knew their teacher would be displeased. What could they do?

One of the girls had an idea. "John," she said, "you are a leader. Our teacher will listen to you. Will you please go to her for us? Tell her what we did. Tell her we are sorry. Tell her we will do whatever she asks."

After some urging from the others, John bravely went to the teacher. John was chosen to go to someone important to ask forgiveness for the wrong his classmates had done.

1. THE PRIESTHOOD: WHAT IT IS
Hebrews 5:1-10; 7:11-28

Priests in the Old Testament had duties similar to the one John had. A priest was chosen to do something for people who had sinned. But he was chosen by *God* to do this important work. And he went to someone more important than a teacher. He went to *God* for the people. A priest had to do his work carefully according to the rules of God.

Show Illustration #1

He had to wear particular kinds of clothing. He had to offer specific gifts and sacrifices to God.

Why do we need to know about priests who lived several thousand years ago? Because the writer of the book of Hebrews says something extremely important about priests. He writes about two different priests in the Old Testament. Then he compares them to the most wonderful Priest–the Lord Jesus Christ who came hundreds of years later. Jesus is the highest Priest of all the Great High Priest. He offered only one sacrifice to God: His own precious blood. That was enough to satisfy God forever. Now Christ is sitting alongside of God in Heaven. He, the Son of God, speaks to God for us. Because Jesus is our Great High Priest, we know God hears our prayers.

It is wonderful that we can talk directly to God asking for His blessing and help. But listen carefully! Near the end of the lesson, you will learn a wonderful secret about yourself.

2. THE REASON FOR THE PRIESTHOOD
Romans 5:12-19

Why did God choose priests? Why were they necessary? For that answer we'll have to start at the very beginning of time.

God created people so He could enjoy their friendship. He wanted to talk with them and be with them. But they soon spoiled things by choosing to sin. This sin caused a great separation to come between people and God. God is holy. People are sinful. Even the very *best* that people can do looks like dirty rags to God. (See Isaiah 64:6.) How awful our *sins* must look to Him!

Think of a enormous valley wider and deeper than any you've ever seen. Man is on one side; God is on the other. No one can jump across the valley: it's too wide. No one can climb down one side and up the other. It's much too deep and there's a raging river below. What is needed to get across the valley? A bridge.

Show Illustration #2

God was so eager to enjoy friendship with people that He provided a bridge that reached between people and Himself. That bridge was the priest. The priest would offer sacrifices on an altar. Those sacrifices would cover man's sin until Christ came to earth. Then He would take the punishment for those sins once for all. The priest would be a man, so he could understand the weakness and sinfulness of mankind. He would carefully follow all of God's rules, offering gifts and sacrifices for sins.

For many years after Adam and Eve sinned, the father of each family served as the family priest. But people soon forgot God and failed to offer their sacrifices for sin. They had no excuse because they knew God was holy. They knew they were sinful. They knew there was a great separation between them and God. Years later the people of Israel begged their leader, Moses, to go to God for them and bring God's message back to them.

3. GOD GIVES A PRIEST TO HIS PEOPLE
Exodus 19:5-8

God called Moses up to Mount Sinai. There God gave him definite laws which the Israelites were to obey. God told Moses He had chosen Aaron (Moses' brother) to be His special priest. Aaron was to be high priest. His sons were to serve as priests also.

God also gave Moses directions for preparing a tabernacle (a movable tent). The tabernacle would be a place to worship God.

Show Illustration #3

Aaron would do his work each day in the tabernacle. At night he would light the golden lamp stand.

Later, when the tabernacle was built, it was filled with God's shining brightness, for God was there. A large cloud rested above it. When the cloud moved, the people of God moved, taking the tabernacle with them.

The tabernacle was divided into two parts. All priests were allowed in the front part, known as the *Holy Place*. But the high priest was the only one ever allowed into the other part of the tabernacle. That was known as the *Holy of Holies* (or *Most Holy Place*). And he could enter only once a year. So, because Aaron was the high priest, he had this special duty and privilege. Once a year he passed beyond the beautiful curtain into the holy of holies, taking with him a blood sacrifice. (See Hebrews 9:7.)

The hundreds of sacrifices offered by the priests each year brought God's people back into fellowship with Him. When blood was shed in the right way by the right person, God's demands were met. He forgave sin and man was allowed to worship God.

God set apart others to help the priests. He chose the tribe of Levi (the Levites) to do the work connected with the tabernacle. There was much to be done especially when the tabernacle had to be moved. Only those who were chosen could go that near to God's glorious presence and live. God is holy and all powerful. Therefore, He has the right to say exactly how sinful man must do things.

4. GOD CONSECRATES HIS PRIESTS
Exodus 28:1–29:46; Leviticus 8:1-36

When God chose the priests and the Levites, He knew He was choosing men who were as sinful as the rest of the people. But God taught Moses exactly how the priests were to be set apart as His special men. Setting the men apart was called consecration.

Show Illustration #4

Moses brought Aaron, God's chosen high priest, to the outer curtain of the tabernacle. There (at the laver) Aaron was completely bathed with water and dressed in the particular clothing God wanted him to wear. Oil was poured on his head to show that God had chosen him for special service. Blood was sprinkled on various parts of his body. This meant that even the parts of his body were being set apart for service to God.

Aaron's being set apart is like the consecration of someone who lives today. And that leads us to the secret E promised to tell you about yourself.

First, we must remember that the Lord Jesus Christ is our Great High Priest. Because He shed His blood for us, we can come into God's holy presence by receiving His gift of forgiveness. (See Hebrews 10:19.) When we receive the Lord Jesus we become members of God's family, children of our Great High Priest. Now this is the wonderful truth about you: The Bible says that *every believer is also a priest to God*. It also says *believers are a royal priesthood*! (See 1 Peter 2:5, 9; Revelation 1:6.) This certainly shows that believers are very special to God.

He chose us before the world was made. (See Ephesians 1:4.) He wants us to be set apart. He wants us to be clean and pure.

Our consecration as priests is much like Aaron's. We must come to the door, not of the tabernacle, but to Jesus the Door. (See John 10:9; Hebrews 10:19-20.) When we place our trust in Him, we are saved. Then we can serve Him. his Word shows us our sinfulness and reminds us to confess our sin (Psalm 119:9, 11; Hebrews 10:22). It is by His shed blood that we are forgiven. By obeying His Word our lives are kept clean and pure (Ephesians 5:26). We are still weak and must confess our sins every day. (See 1 John 1:9.) We must keep ourselves unspotted from sin. (See James 1:27.)

Like the Old Testament priests, even the parts of our body are to be useful and set apart to serve God. Can you think of ways to use your hands, your mouth, your feet, your ears for the Lord?

As a priest you do not offer animal sacrifices. When Jesus died, He forever removed the need for that. But your priestly work is like that of the Old Testament priest: you go to God and pray for the people. You are to bring people to God. You pray for others and tell them of God's wonderful way of salvation through Jesus. God wants every believer to do this.

Then you can offer the Lord two sacrifices each day. (1) "Offer the sacrifice of praise to God continually . . . giving thanks to His name." And (2) "Do good and share with others. This is an offering of love to the Lord for with such sacrifices God is well pleased." (See Hebrews 13:15-16.)

Will you thank God for setting you apart to serve Him? Will you ask Him to show you how you can serve Him in a special way this week? Will you promise to praise Him continually?

Lesson 2
THE PRIESTHOOD OF MELCHIZEDEK

NOTE TO THE TEACHER

God established the Aaronic priesthood at about the same time He gave His covenant to Israel. Therefore it is difficult to divide these two subjects into separate volumes. For example, God's covenant with Israel depended upon the blood of a sacrifice. Sacrificial blood was also required for the priest to go into God's presence.

Similar principles will be taught in this volume and in the next (*The Covenant*). Do not be afraid to repeat principles. An idea presented in two different settings enlarges our understanding of Biblical truths. Ask the Holy Spirit to guide you and teach you as you prepare these lessons, teacher.

Review the previous lesson by giving your students opportunity to tell what sacrifices they offered to God. Did they praise Him even in difficulties? Did they pray for others? Did they introduce others to the Lord Jesus? Did they show kindnesses to others? Did they share any of their possessions with others?

Remember: A lesson is not learned until it is lived. Bible truths must affect each life–student's and teacher's.

Scripture to be studied: Genesis 14:17-20; Numbers 16:1, 17:13; 26:9-11; 2 Chronicles 26:1-21; Hebrews 5:5-10; 6:20 7:28

The *aim* of the lesson: To show the superiority of Christ's priesthood.

What your students should *know*: Christ has an eternal priesthood.

What your students should *feel*: A desire to serve God as royal priests.

What your students should *do*: Praise God for the eternal priesthood of Christ; determine to introduce others to Him.

Lesson outline (for the teacher's and students' notebooks):

1. God punishes His sinful set-apart ones (Leviticus 10:1-2).
2. The service of a priest is holy (Numbers 16:1-17:13).
3. Melchizedek's priesthood pleased God (Genesis 14:17-20).
4. Christ is a priest forever after the order of Melchizedek (Hebrews 5:5-10; 6:20-7:28).

The verse to be memorized:

Seeing then that we have a great High Priest, that is passed into the heavens, Jesus, the Son of God, let us hold fast our profession. (Hebrews 4:14)

THE LESSON

Suppose you absolutely must have a certain thing. (*Teacher:* Name an article of food or clothing your students might need.) Without it, you cannot live another day. You must have it now. You have relatives who would be glad to share with you, if they knew your need. What should you do? (Allow class discussion, please.) The answer to this question depends on whether or not you are a member of the family of God. If you have not trusted in the Lord Jesus Christ, then you are not a child of God. So you will probably have to ask your relatives to help you. But if you have received Christ as your Saviour, God is your heavenly Father. That means you have a Great High Priest who is asking God right now to care for you. Who is the Christian believer's Great High Priest? (The Lord Jesus Christ.)

"God shall supply all your need," the Bible tells us. (See Philippians 4:19.) The Lord Jesus said, "Whatever you shall ask the Father in My name, He will give it you . . . Ask [in My name], and you shall receive, that your joy may be full." (See John 16:23-24.)

These are tremendous promises. But God and the Lord Jesus are in Heaven hundreds, thousands, maybe millions of miles away! And the thing you need must be in your hand this very day. Does distance affect God? If you could hear Christ praying for you in the next room, would you expect an immediate answer? Yes, you certainly would. Remember! The distance makes no difference. The Lord Jesus *is* praying for you. And God knows exactly what you need and when. If we ask anything according to His will, He hears us. And if we know He hears us, we know we will receive what we ask Him for. (Have class read 1 John 5:14-15.) Why can Christian believers have such a wonderful promise? Because the Lord Jesus Christ is their Great High Priest in Heaven.

Long, long before the Lord Jesus came to earth, God provided earthly priests for his people. God said, "Moses, set apart your brother Aaron and his sons from the rest of the people. I have chosen them to be priests unto Me." (God gave this command at the time He gave Moses the Law and the instructions for building the tabernacle.)

We are not told why God chose Aaron and his sons to be priests. But because He chose them, they became His special servants.

Show Illustration #1

They wore a particular kind of clothing, ordered by God Himself. They offered specific gifts and sacrifices to God.

Show Illustration #2

Those earthly priests were like a bridge between sinful mankind and God, the holy One. The animal sacrifices the priests offered *covered* the sins of those who brought the sacrifices. This made it possible for the sinner to worship God. But if he had brought even a thousand sacrifices, his sins would not have been *taken away*. (See Hebrews 10:4, 11.) However, when God the Son offered His own blood on the cross, no more sacrifices for sins were needed. (See Hebrews 10:10-18.) Not then. Not now. Not ever. Only by Christ alone can sinners now come to God.

Show Illustration #3

The earthly priests of long ago had special work to do. God told them clearly what their responsibilities were.

Show Illustration #4

The men whom God chose as priests were set apart from the rest of the people by God Himself. Setting the men apart was called consecration.

(*Teacher:* In reviewing lesson #1, it would be best to question the students. Allow them to explain the meanings of the illustration.)

At first, fathers of families were priests. Later, Aaron and his sons were the priests. They confessed their own sins and the sins of the people. They offered animal sacrifices for those sins. Years afterward, the Lord Jesus Christ offered His *own* blood. That was the perfect sacrifice for all sins forever. Now He is in Heaven sitting beside God the Father. He, the Great High Priest, is praying for His own.

Today, each one who has trusted in Christ is also a priest. But believer-priests do not offer animal sacrifices. Instead, they offer sacrifices of praise to God. They do good. They share with others. They pray for others. They introduce others to the Son of God. They are expected to live lives that are clean and pure.

1. GOD PUNISHES HIS SINFUL SET-APART ONES
Leviticus 10:1-2

Do present-day priests always live clean, pure lives? Do they always share with others? Are they always good and kind? No, they often fail. Priests in the long ago failed, too. Some priests forgot God. Others deliberately turned away from Him. They had to be punished. Aaron's own sons disobeyed God's rules about offerings they were to make to Him. They were immediately punished with death. (See Leviticus 10:1-2.) It was–and is!–a serious thing to be a priest of God.

God had chosen the Levites to help the priests in the tabernacle work. Because He had set them apart for himself, He wanted their lives to honor Him. Certain Levites did not like their work of helping the high priest. One of them, Korah, wanted to be the high priest. Proudly he told Moses and Aaron: "You take too much upon yourself. You are no better than anyone else. God has chosen all of us as His special people."

Moses answered, "In the morning the Lord will show whom He has chosen as His priest. God has chosen you from among all the people of Israel to be near Himself as you do your work in the tabernacle. Does it seem a small thing to you that God has given this task to you Levites only? You want to be priests also. You are revolting against the Lord God. Come here tomorrow before the Lord–you and your men."

The next day Moses announced to all the people: "If the Lord does a miracle and the ground splits open and swallows these men, then you will know that they have despised the Lord God."

Show Illustration #5

Immediately the earth opened and swallowed Korah, his men, their tents, their families, their friends. Everything they owned was gone. The earth closed up and they were dead. (See Numbers 16:1-35; Jude 11.)

When God chooses anyone to do His work, He expects that person to do what He asks. If the one God chose is jealous of another, God will deal with that person–severely, perhaps.

2. THE SERVICE OF A PRIEST IS HOLY
Numbers 16:1 17:13

There were two kings who felt they could do anything they wanted, even the work of the priests. They knew God had set apart priests to go between sinful men and God, the holy One. But they thought more of what they themselves wanted, rather than what God had ordered. (See 1 Samuel 13:1-14 for the account of King Saul's sin.)

Show Illustration #6

King Uzziah began as a good king. He did what God wanted and God made him successful. But the day came when he was proud of his strength. With self-importance he pushed past the priests and marched into the temple of the Lord. There he burned incense upon the altar. The priests rushed in after him, demanding that he get out. "This is the work of the priests alone!" they shouted. "Priests are consecrated (set apart) to burn incense. Get out! The Lord God will not honor you for doing this!"

King Uzziah was furious. He refused to leave the holy place. And immediately leprosy appeared on his forehead. The Lord God had struck him. So King Uzziah, a leper, lived alone cut off from everyone until he died. It was clear for all to see that the priesthood which God had established was holy.

3. MELCHIZEDEK'S PRIESTHOOD PLEASED GOD
Genesis 14:17-20

The Hebrew people who received the Bible letter addressed to them had much to think about that. The Spirit of God had shown them that His Son is greater than everything that was important to them. He is better than Jewish prophets. He is better than angels. He is better than Moses, their great leader. He is better than the holy priesthood of Aaron. Five times in the letter to the Hebrews God says that the Lord Jesus is a Priest forever after the order of Melchizedek. (See Hebrews 5:6, 10; 6:20; 7:17, 21; compare Psalm 110:4.)

The Hebrews remembered Melchizedek. He lived long before Aaron and the Levites. Melchizedek (his name means *king of righteousness*) was the king of Salem (later called Jerusalem). He was a good king. Because he pleased God, God chose him to be a priest also.

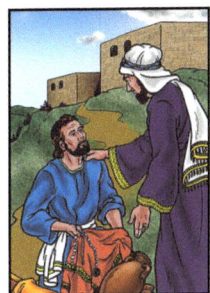

Show Illustration #7

The father of the Jewish people, Abraham, met Melchizedek one day. Abraham was on his way home from winning a battle. He was carrying many good things which he had captured from the enemy. King Melchizedek the priest brought God's blessing to Abraham. In turn, Abraham gave one-tenth of his goods to the king-priest, the servant of God. In so doing, Abraham was confessing that Melchizedek was greater than he (Abraham), the father of the Jews.

4. CHRIST IS A PRIEST FOREVER AFTER THE ORDER OF MELCHIZEDEK
Hebrews 5:5-10; 6:20–7:28

It is not surprising then that God told the Hebrew Christians that Jesus, our Great High Priest, is similar to Melchizedek. God chose Melchizedek because Melchizedek pleased Him. God chose His own Son to be the Great High Priest because Jesus pleased Him. Melchizedek was both a king and a priest. Our Lord Jesus is also King and Priest. He was born of the royal family of David. He offered His own precious blood as the perfect sacrifice for the sins of all people forever. He is the Great High Priest.

From the very beginning when Adam sinned, man was separated from God by sin. Later, God gave His people a tabernacle, then a temple. In each there was a heavy curtain (the veil), which kept the people away from God's holy presence.

Show Illustration #8

When the Lord Jesus Christ died on the cross, God tore the veil from the top to the bottom. Days later Jesus ascended to Heaven. God the Father said, "Sit here at My right hand until I make You King over everyone." (See Hebrews 1:13.) And there He sits today, the Great High Priest, praying for His own.

Like Melchizedek, the Lord Jesus brings blessings to God's people. If you are a Christian believer, He blesses you. If you are a member of the family of the Royal Priest, you are a royal priest to God. Imagine that!

You are invited to come fearlessly into God's holy presence with your praises and requests. Some day you will reign with Him forever. But right now, He deserves your loving service. What can you do this week to prove that you are praising him, that you love Him?

(*Teacher:* Allow time for answers then have prayer, allowing each to dedicate himself/herself to the Lord and His service.)

Lesson 3
THE WORK OF THE HIGH PRIEST

NOTE TO THE TEACHER

The Old Testament priesthood presents many beautiful pictures of the work of the Lord Jesus. For example: Aaron had on the shoulders of his priestly garments two precious onyx stones–stones which shone like fire. Each had engraved upon it the names of six of the twelve tribes of Israel. When Aaron went before the Lord, he always carried on his shoulders (the place of strength) the names of these tribes. He also wore a breastplate covering his heart. In the breastplate were twelve precious stones. Each had the name of one of the tribes engraved on it. He wore their names upon his heart, continually reminding God of His people. (See Exodus 28:12, 29.) The strength of the priest's shoulders and the affections of his heart were reserved for those whom he served.

So it is with our Great High Priest, the Lord Jesus Christ. He bears us up on His shoulders and on His heart, as He appears before the throne of God continually. We are safe on the shoulders of Him, who is the Mighty God. We have no need to worry about anything. He tells us to cast all our cares upon Him for He cares for us. (See 1 Peter 5:7.)

Scripture to be studied: Leviticus 16:1-34; 23:26-32; Hebrews 9:1-28

The *aim* of the lesson: To show the work which the Lord Jesus has done, is doing and will do for us.

  What your students should *know*: Christ lives forever to pray for His own (Hebrews 7:25).

  What your students should *feel*: The importance of keeping their lives clean.

  What your students should *do*: Prepare their lives for the coming of the Lord Jesus.

Lesson outline (for the teacher's and students' notebooks):
1. The Day of Atonement (Leviticus 16:1-34; 23:26-32).
2. Christ offered one sacrifice for us (Hebrews 9:25-26).
3. Christ is in the presence of God for us (Hebrews 9:24).
4. Christ will come again for us (Hebrews 9:27-28).

The verse to be memorized:

Seeing then that we have a great High Priest, that is passed into the heavens, Jesus, the Son of God, let us hold fast our profession. (Hebrews 4:14)

THE LESSON
1. THE DAY OF ATONEMENT
Leviticus 16:1-34; 23:26-32

What did young children do and say hundreds of years ago when Aaron was the high priest? Could it have been like this?

Two boys raced across the hot desert sand. They ran around one tent after another. Tired from their running, they dropped in the shade of a tent. Iddo panted, "Everyone looks busy. They must be getting ready for the Day of Atonement."

Uzzi answered, "Yes, Father and the other priests have been talking about that special day. They say we must not do any work then. We must be sad for our sins. It is the day when atonement is made for our sins. Do you know what atonement means?"

Iddo said, "My father said it means our sins are covered over for another year. God cannot stay where there is sin, because He is holy. He will be with us in the middle of our camp for another year when atonement has been made for our sins."

Uzzi said, "I do not understand how God can be here in our camp and in Heaven at the same time."

Iddo replied, "Father says God is Spirit. That means He has no body and can be *everywhere* at the *same* time. He lives in Heaven, that is true. But He is right here in our camp as well. It is hard to understand. But He can do it because He is God."

Uzzi suggested, "Let us go over to the tabernacle and ask Grandfather to tell us more about it."

They found Uzzi's grandfather outside the tabernacle talking to one of the priests. Seeing the boys, he asked kindly, "What do you want?"

"Grandfather, will you please tell us about the Day of Atonement? We do not understand much about it from last year. We were too young then," Uzzi said.

Show Illustration #9

"I have time before I must kill the evening sacrifice," Grandfather answered. "Shall we sit in the shade of those tents?"

When they were all seated, Grandfather continued. "The tenth day of the seventh month is the time God set aside for a day of sorrow for sin. Every year on that date we must confess our sins so they can be covered. Atonement means *to cover*. Our sins which separate us from God (the holy, righteous One) are covered by the blood of animal sacrifices on the Day of Atonement. We must make atonement for the tabernacle and its many parts, also for the priests, the Levites and all the people. Our sins cause everything around us to be unclean."

"What does the high priest do on the Day of Atonement?" Uzzi asked.

Grandfather answered, "Early that morning he must slay a young bull and a ram. He offers them for his sins and those of his family. He bathes himself and puts on special garments that are kept for the Day of Atonement. He will go inside the veil into the *Holy of Holies* (or *Most Holy Place*). This is the only time during the year that he is allowed to go directly into the presence of God.

"No one else is ever allowed to enter the most holy place. The high priest must take a blood sacrifice with him. When he goes inside the veil (a beautiful curtain), he puts incense on hot coals. This causes a sweet smelling cloud to cover the mercy seat where God is. The priest sprinkles the blood on the mercy seat and in front of it for his own sins. Then he goes out again to make a sacrifice for the sins of the people. This is the way God says it must be done on the Day of Atonement."

"I heard people talking about using two goats. Why do they use two goats?" Iddo asked.

"After the high priest comes from the holy place, he brings two goats to the door of the tabernacle. One goat is chosen to be the Lord's. The other is to be sent away. The Lord's goat is sacrificed as a sin offering. Its blood is taken inside the veil. It is sprinkled on the ground and on the mercy seat. The priest makes atonement for the tabernacle, the altar and the holy place. He also makes atonement for his own sins and the sins of his people.

"Then he comes out again and lays both hands on the head of the living goat. While doing this, he confesses the sins of the people of Israel. This places their sins onto the head of the living goat. We may not understand this, but God told us to do it. It is His way of covering our sins for another year. The goat is let loose in the wild desert to wander where no one lives. This reminds us that God forgives our sins and forgets them."

"The high priest returns into the tabernacle. He takes off the special garments, bathes and puts on his beautiful priestly garments again. When he comes out, he makes other sacrifices to please God. They are called burnt offerings."

"And that is why God can be in our camp," said Uzzi. "It is cleansed and kept holy because of the sacrifices for sin. It is wonderful to have a Day of Atonement each year!"

2. CHRIST OFFERED ONE SACRIFICE FOR US
Hebrews 9:25-26

Show Illustration #10

The Day of Atonement was full of activities that seem unusual–even strange –to us. But we must learn about that day so we can better understand Christ's work as our Great High Priest.

The high priest on the Day of Atonement appeared in three different places: (1) He was outside the tabernacle, slaying the animals and offering their blood as sacrifices for sin. (2) He was inside the veil, in God's presence in the most holy place. There he offered incense and sprinkled the blood. (3) Then he came out again, alive, showing that God had accepted the sacrifices for sin.

Like the Old Testament priest, Christ also appears in three different places: (1) Hebrews 9 says *He came to earth* to put away sin (v. 26) by a better sacrifice the sacrifice of Himself. This sacrifice never needs to be repeated, not once a year, not ever. (See Hebrews 2:14-15.) The offering of Jesus' blood paid *the penalty* for sin. It pleased God completely and forever. God never remembers the believer's sins any more. (See Hebrews 8:12; 10:17.) For Uzzi and those who lived before Christ came, it was wonderful to have a Day of Atonement each year. But it is even more wonderful for us today. We have a High Priest who died once and never needs to die again. When our trust is in Him (the Lord Jesus), our sins are forgiven forever!

3. CHRIST IS IN THE PRESENCE OF GOD FOR US
Hebrews 9:24

(2) *The second appearance* of the Lord Jesus is in *the very presence* of God. Christ is there right now.

Show Illustration #11

The Old Testament high priest went through a veil into the most holy place of the tabernacle with incense and animal blood as a sacrifice for sin. But the Lord Jesus offered His *own* blood. Then, because God accepted His sacrifice, Christ rose again and went into Heaven. There He is now in God's own presence praying for us. He tells God that our sins have been paid for. He asks God to forgive us and cleanse us whenever we break our fellowship by sinning again. Jesus is there in Heaven praying that we will not fail when we are tested. He wants us to be free from *the power of sin*. But, if we should fail Him, He pleads for us. And His blood cleanses us and keeps us safe. (See 1 John 1:7, 9; 2:1-2.)

4. CHRIST WILL COME AGAIN FOR US
Hebrews 9:27-28

Show Illustration #12

The Old Testament priest came out from God's presence in glory and beauty. Jesus has yet to make *His third appearance*. But it will be in greater glory and beauty than the world has ever known. Today Jesus sits at God's right hand.

(3) Some day–it could be today!–Christ will appear again. He will break through the skies and catch all believers up from this sinful world. Each Christian's body will be changed so it will be gloriously like Christ's. When He comes for us, we shall leave behind us all temptation, sin, weakness, sickness and sadness. We shall be forever free *from the presence of sin* and forever happy with the Lord Jesus Christ.

Does it thrill you to think of Christ's coming for His own? It should if you are a Christian. If you are not a Christian, will you come to Him in prayer today, confessing your sins and asking Christ to be your Saviour?

The Bible says that Christians who are looking forward to the coming of the Lord Jesus, those who love His appearing, will receive a crown. (See 2 Timothy 4:8.)

Will you be ashamed or embarrassed when He comes? You will be if your life is not clean.

Are you doing each day what a believer-priest is supposed to do? Are you praising Him? bringing others to Him? praying for others? doing deeds of love for others? Perhaps you need to ask His forgiveness for some things that are displeasing to Him. Perhaps you need to get busy telling others about the Lord Jesus. Or maybe you need to become more faithful in reading His Word, praying, going to church. Perhaps you need to show more love to your family, your friends–even your enemies. The Bible says Jesus is coming. If He should come today, will you be ready to meet Him?

List in your notebook the things you want to do this week –whatever you want to have done when the Lord Jesus comes for His own.

Lesson 4
CHRIST IS OUR GREAT HIGH PRIEST

NOTE TO THE TEACHER

As we close these studies on the priesthood of Christ, do we appreciate Him more each day? He has given us eternal life. We shall never perish. No one can pluck us out of His hand.

He is our life. The Apostle Paul said, "I live; yet not I, but Christ lives in me" (Galatians 2:20). If our lives are fully surrendered to Him, we will be kind and loving to others. Can we be too busy to do something for Him each day? Remember! He said, "When you have done good to one of the least of my brothers, you have done it unto Me."

We finish our lesson today far above the problems of earth. We are standing before the throne of the Lamb of God. Listen as we hear the praise ascending to Him: "Thou art worthy, O Lord, to receive glory and honor and power: for Thou hast created all things, and for Thy pleasure they are and were created" (Revelation 4:11). This is a beautiful song of praise in which we should join.

There is something better, however, for which we shall praise Him in that coming day. We shall praise Him for redeeming us by His blood. (See Revelation 5:9-12.) We shall praise Him for making us kings and priests before our God. We shall praise Him for declaring us in right standing with God. We shall adore Him for His faithfulness in keeping us from falling, for presenting us faultless before God. (See Jude 24.) Words do not seem to be enough to express the love and gratitude we feel for our Great High Priest. But He understands even our inability to praise Him as we wish to do. He has given us His Spirit to live within us. He helps us overcome our weaknesses. He helps us pray even when words fail us. He helps us as we serve God as His priests on earth.

Scripture to be studied: Luke 10:30-37; references in Hebrews as used in lesson

The *aim* of the lesson: To show the character of Christ, our Great High Priest.

  What your students should *know*: They have One to whom they can go for help in every trouble.

  What your students should *feel*: A desire to follow the example of our Great High Priest.

  What your students should *do*: Offer the sacrifice of praise to God right now.

Lesson outline (for the teacher's and students' notebooks):
1. A priest is to be kind, loving and good (Luke 10:30-37).
2. Our Great High Priest: the example of kindness and love (Hebrews 2:14-18; 4:15-16; 5:7-9; 13:1-3).
3. Our Great High Priest lives forever to help us (Hebrews 2:17; 7:25).
4. Our Great High Priest is worthy of all our praise (Revelation 5:9, 12-13).

The verse to be memorized:

Seeing then that we have a great High Priest, that is passed into the heavens, Jesus, the Son of God, let us hold fast our profession. (Hebrews 4:14)

THE LESSON
1. A PRIEST IS TO BE KIND, LOVING AND GOOD
Luke 10:30-37

When the Lord Jesus looked upon the people who crowded around Him, He felt great pity for them. He saw them wandering carelessly as sheep wander without a shepherd.

Hebrews 5:2 tells us that a priest should be like the Lord Jesus. He should be kind and have pity for those who are going the wrong way. Priests in Bible times knew it was hard to live to please God. They had been chosen and set apart by God for His service. Yet they were often tempted by Satan. They were to be shepherds of the Israelite people, leading them to God. Instead, many times they went the wrong way themselves. The priests and Levites often forgot that their duties included loving the people.

When Jesus Christ lived on earth as a man, He showed by His life what a true priest should be. Once He told a story to show the kind of love and pity a real priest should have. He said that a man was walking on a lonely road from Jerusalem to Jericho. Suddenly a thief jumped out from a hiding place and grabbed him. He tore the man's clothes and snatched his money pouch.

"Help! Someone, help!" the poor man screamed. "He's going to kill me!" The robber struck him, knocking him to the ground.

The man collapsed, half dead. And the robber escaped. Later, a priest came along. "Help me! Help me!" the injured man sobbed. Surely the priest knew it was his duty to show pity. He knew he should help. But he walked right past the man.

The next to come along was a Levite. He walked closer to the wounded man. He stopped, but only for a moment. He did not touch the man. He did not examine him. He did not offer to help. He simply walked on.

Show Illustration #13

Another man came. He was not a priest from Aaron's family. Nor was he from the tribe of Levi. He was a Samaritan. (Samaritans and Jews disliked each other.) The Samaritan thought, *This could have happened to me. I hope he is alive.*

He treated the stranger as if he was his own brother. He carefully washed the wounds with oil. He wrapped them with strips of cloth. With kindness, he lifted the suffering man, put him on his donkey and took him to an inn. The battered man, after he recovered, could have worked to pay for his lodging. But his new friend would not allow that.

Show Illustration #14

The Samaritan gave up his own plans. He stayed with the injured man all night. He paid the inn-keeper for the man's lodging. The friend had the kind of love that pleases God, because he kept on giving.

Show Illustration #15

The next day he had to leave to take care of his own business. He could not stay longer with the wounded man. So he did a wonderful thing. He paid the innkeeper to nurse him back to health. Then he promised, "I shall return later. I will repay whatever you spend for his care."

Were the priests and Levites who heard this story, ashamed? *They* were the ones who were to have pity. *They* were supposed to be loving and kind. Instead, it was the stranger who did what they should have done.

2. OUR GREAT HIGH PRIEST: THE EXAMPLE OF KINDNESS AND LOVE
Hebrews 2:14-18; 4:15-16; 5:7-9; 13:1-3

In the book of Hebrews we read that our Great High Priest showed His loving-kindness toward us. He, the Creator of the universe, took to Himself a body. He came to live on earth as a man. Although He is the Mighty God, He allowed Himself to be tested, as we are. (See Hebrews 2:14-18; 4:15.) Even though He is God the Son, He suffered and died to redeem us. (See Hebrews 5:7-9.) He walked the road of life. Always He loved and helped those who were in need. And now, today, He invites us to come to Him boldly for His help in our time of need. (See Hebrews 4:16.) He wants us to help others in need. He wants us to be kind and loving, even to strangers.

The Bible reminds us that all Christians are our brothers and sisters. We are to treat them with love. (Review Illustration #14.) We are to do kind things for them and pray for them. We are to be content with our own things. (See Hebrews 13:1-3.) As we love others, we please God.

3. OUR GREAT HIGH PRIEST LIVES FOREVER TO HELP US
Hebrews 2:17; 7:25

Show Illustration #15

The kind friend in Jesus story gave his word that he would keep right on helping the man who had been robbed.

Just so, the Lord Jesus gives His word that He will always care for us. He is God the Son. He bore our sins on the cross and arose from the dead. Now He lives forever to help us. In Hebrews we read, "He is able to save completely and forever those who come to God by Him, because He lives forever to pray for them." (See Hebrews 7:25.) Christ is our understanding, faithful High Priest. (See Hebrews 2:17.) Now, and for as long as we need Him, He cares for us who have trusted in Him. He helps us when we are sick. He gives us strength to work for Him. He answers our problems.

4. OUR GREAT HIGH PRIEST IS WORTHY OF ALL OUR PRAISE
Revelation 5:9, 12-13

Show Illustration #16

Because Christ is perfect, His priesthood never changes. It is always holy and pure and perfect. The Lord Jesus Christ pleases God in every way. Today He is sitting beside God the Father in Heaven. Some future day the Lord Jesus will reign as King. In His Kingdom everything will be absolutely right. Everyone will be given what he deserves. If a Christian believer has done nothing on earth for his Saviour, he will not be rewarded in Heaven. But a good worker will receive rewards. He wants us to be good priests.

He wants us to stay true to Him. He wants us to bring others to Him. He expects us to praise Him and do kind things for others. Then, when life is over, we shall stand before Him. And He will reward us for *all* we did to please Him. There is even a reward for those who are looking for His coming. Imagine that!

What will we do with our rewards, our crowns? We will lay them at Jesus feet. (See Revelation 4:10.) We will worship Him and praise Him for being our faithful and righteous High Priest. Listen to the praise that all who have put their trust in Christ will give to Him:

"Thou art worthy . . . for Thou wast slain and hast redeemed us to God by Thy blood out of every . . . people and nation; and hast made us unto our God kings and priests . . . Worthy is the Lamb that was slain . . . Blessing, and honor, and glory, and power be unto Him who sits upon the throne . . . (See Revelation 5:9, 12-13.)

Surely One who is so great, deserves all our worship and praise right now. As we bow our heads to pray, will you thank Him for something He has done for you? Will you thank Him for being your faithful High Priest? You may pray aloud if you wish, or silently in your heart.

(***Teacher:*** Did you feel the thrill of that last Scripture in Revelation? If so, and if it showed in your voice and on your face, some of your students may have caught it too and will be bursting with praise. Give them opportunity to pray briefly, one after the other. If they are bashful, you can pray and then have them join in one of their favorite songs of praise. They will doubtless sing heartily.)